Penguin Books

The 101 Best and

G000127614

Spike Milligan wa

1918. He received

Hyderabad Sindh

through a series of Roman Catholic schools in India
and England, to the Lewisham Polytechnic. Always
something of a playboy, he then plunged into the world
of Show Business, seduced by his first stage appear-
ance, at the age of eight, in the nativity play of his
Poona convent school. He began his career as a band
musician but has since become famous as a humorous
script-writer and actor in both films and broadcasting.
He was one of the main figures in and behind the in-
famous Goon Show. Among the films he has appeared
in are: *Suspect*, *Invasion*, *Postman's Knock* and
Milligan at Large.

Spike Milligan's published work includes *The Little
Potboiler*, *Silly Verse for Kids*, *Dustbin of Milligan*, *A
Book of Bits*, *The Bed-Sitting Room* (a play), *The Bald
Twit Lion*, *A Book of Milliganimals*, *Small Dreams of
a Scorpion*, *Transports of Delight*, *The Milligan Book
of Records*, *Games, Cartoons and Commercials*, *Dip
the Puppy*, *William McGonagall: The Truth at Last*
(with Jack Hobbs), *The Spike Milligan Letters* and
More Spike Milligan Letters, both edited by Norma
Farnes, *Open Heart University*, *The Q Annual*, *Unspun
Socks from a Chicken's Laundry*, *There's a Lot of
It About*, *The Melting Pot*, *Puckoon* and *Further
Transports of Delight*. His unique and incomparable six
volumes of war memoirs are: *Adolf Hitler: My Part in
His Downfall*, *'Rommel?' 'Gunner Who?'*, *Monty: His
Part in My Victory*, *Mussolini: His Part in My
Downfall*, *Where Have All the Bullets Gone?* and
Goodbye, Soldier.

PENGUIN BOOKS

Published by the Penguin Group
27 Wrights Lane, London W8 5TZ, England
Viking Penguin Inc., 40 West 23rd Street, New York, New York 10010, USA
Penguin Books Australia Ltd, Ringwood, Victoria, Australia
Penguin Books Canada Ltd, 2801 John Street, Markham, Ontario, Canada L3R 1B4
Penguin Books (NZ) Ltd, 182–190 Wairau Road, Auckland 10, New Zealand

Penguin Books Ltd, Registered Offices: Harmondsworth, Middlesex, England

First published in Great Britain by M & J Hobbs and Michael Joseph 1982
Published in Penguin Books 1988
10 9 8 7 6 5 4 3 2 1

Printed and bound in Great Britain by
Cox & Wyman Ltd, Reading

I dedicate this book to my last book
Indefinite Articles and Scunthorpe
which didn't do very well.
I also dedicate it to Harry Secombe's suit
which has been under great pressure
for the last three years.

Sir Harry Secombe is now appearing at the
Odeon at Kuala Lumpur which is a
pity because it has been closed
for the last twenty years.

How did he get a knighthood when I've only
just been made a mister?

The 101 Best and Only Limericks of Spike Milligan

SPIKE MILLIGAN

Illustrations by DESMOND MILLIGAN

PENGUIN BOOKS

There was a young man from Blighty
Who wore a transparent nightie.
The vicar said, 'Son,
It's really not done,
It's not wrong – but it's also not rightie.'

A lady called Adelaide Rose
Went around without any clothes.
She had a slim figure
But as she got bigger
She had much more to disclose.

A man who moved to Australia
Said, 'Please readdress all my mail here
Care of Box 29
Newcastle-on-Tyne.'
No wonder it all was a failure.

There was an old perve from Leeds
Who had a thing about beads.
He would sew them on clothes,
Some he'd stuff up his nose –
It seemed to suffice all his needs.

A very sick man from Bled
Arose every dawn from his bed.
He worked twelve hours a day
Without food, without pay.
Surprise, surprise – he's dead.

A girl from a nice convent school
Was wicked, sadistic and cruel.
One night, just for fun,
She set fire to a nun,
Screaming, 'Oh what a silly old fuel.'

A man called J. Arthur Rank
Bought a yacht from a millionaire Yank.
'It's the safest yet built,
Insured to the hilt.'
It made no difference – it sank.

A camel who had two humps
Thought he had got the mumps.
A doctor called Murray
Said, 'Camel, don't worry,
They're not mumps, they're two lumps caused by thumps.'

A man with a mania for owls
Stands in a tree and he howls.
He's been up that tree
Since Nineteen-O-Three
And not once had the use of his bowels.

The Duke of Wellington said,
'This army must be led.'
He said, 'Follow me, men,
We will beat them again
Just as soon as I get out of bed.'

A man from out of space
Said, 'I'm from a superior race.
You're all inferior
While I am superior.'
Then he tripped and fell flat on his face.

A combustible woman from Thang
Exploded one day with a Bang!
The maid then rushed in
And said with a grin,
'Pardon me, madam – you rang?'

King James to his servant said, 'Pray,
Pray what is the time of the day?'
The servant said, 'Oh!
Ying tong iddle I po.'
Then slowly walked away.

Oh what a terrible beast
Is the frog – the frog from the East,
Not the frog from the West
Who walks round in a vest
With his knickers all mangled and creased.

A detective who worked in a store
Caught a thief stealing knickers galore.
To arrest her he had to,
This one he was glad to –
'Twas his grotty old mother-in-law.

A man caught stealing a tree
Told the judge – 'I need it, you see.
My leg needs support.
If it weren't for this court
I'd be walking around quite free.'

A judge named Sir Denning-Manfred
To a County Court jury once said,
'Your verdict should be
G–U–I–L–T
VW–X–Y–Z.'

A man whose mind went blank
Caught a cab on the end of the rank.
Said the cabby, 'Where to?'
He said, 'China will do –
So you'd better top up your tank.'

There was a young man from Ealing
Who decided to walk on the ceiling.
He stood in the hall
And walked up the wall,
Ended up on his back face-down kneeling.

There was a young lady from Brum
Who had an enormous thumb.
The thumb was a curse
But to make matters worse
She had a very big bum.

There was a young man from Mongolia
Said, 'Who's dug this ruddy great hole here?'
Up popped an old man,
He said, 'It's me – Dan –
I'm chasing a ruddy great mole here.'

A carpenter in Finlandia
Said, 'How long have I got to stand here?
I'm all by myself,
Trying to put up a shelf.
Won't somebody give me a hand here?'

A man with a very fast car
Said, 'I'm faster than you, dear papa.'
His father said, 'Right,
I'll race you tonight.'
He did – he beat him – ha! ha!

At dawn as a bugle blew muster
Up galloped the bold General Custer.
From his feet to his crust
He was covered in dust –
He said, 'Somebody lend me a duster.'

There was a young lady of Rye
Who anxiously looked at the sky.
When it fell on her head
It struck her down dead.
Oh, dearie me – dearie my!

There was a young man of Rangoon
Who locked himself up in his room.
When the police with a shout
Said, 'When will you come out?'
'Not today – not tomorrow – but soon!'

A priest in old Donegal
Said, 'Oh no, not at all, not at all.'
Now that's all he said
Till the day he was dead –
And he thought he was having a ball!

A man called Mad Dan McGrew
Was boiling a cauldron of stew.
For no reason at all
He dived in, clothes and all.
Now if he can – why then can't you?

There was a bad man in Madrid
Who was chased by the police – so he hid.
He hid all the day
In a sewer, they say –
That's why he was covered in shid.

There was a young man from Italy
Who was crying and crying quite bitterly.
When people said, 'Why,
Oh why do you cry?'
'Because,' he said, 'someone's just hit-a-me!'

A man with an index-linked nose
Said, 'Look how the damned thing grows.
It keeps swelling as well,
By this you can tell
How the rate of inflation goes.'

There was a young man of Rhyl
Who tried very hard to get ill.
He tried to get scabies,
Bronchitis and rabies,
But all he got was a chill.

A man once decided to test
The shrinkage of his woollen vest.
It was washed in cold water
And it shouldn't oughter –
That's why it's halfway up his chest.

A man called Vincent Van Gogh
Developed an ear-splitting cough.
No sleep could he get
And he wouldn't have yet
Had he not lopped the other ear off.

There was a young man of Rangoon –
I'm sure that he came from Rangoon.
It wasn't Calcutta,
That's right – not Calcutta,
Yes, I'm sure that he came from Rangoon.

A Scotsman from old Aberdeen
Wore clothes so old they were green.
He had good clothes galore
That he just never wore –
I suppose you can call the man mean.

A man who banked at Coutts
Was in rags and had no boots.
When he asked for a loan
They let out a groan
Because banks don't care two bloody hoots!

A man who played a bassoon
Continually played the same tune
Through August to September,
November, December,
March, April, May and now June!

A sailor who sailed round Cape Hope
Pulled ashore to borrow some soap.
He used it for hours
In the bath and the showers
But did he return it? – Nope!

A man who went round with no trousers
At night walked around people's houses.
He was a pervert
For stuffed up his shirt
Guess what? – old ladies' blouses.

A homeopath from Darjeeling
Was dedicated to healing.
But now at one stroke
He's bankrupt – he's broke
'Cause he never charged more than one sheeling.

There was a young man from Calcutta
Who developed a terrible stutter.
The day that he died
People stood round and cried.
Goo–Goo–Goo–Good–b–b–b–bye was all he could mutter.

There was a young man from Berlin
Who had prayed that Hitler would win.
Now he's cleaning the shoes
Of the Golders Green Jews.
Have they got it in for him!

A photographer born with three legs
Took photos and developed the negs.
Each picture he'd take
With one leg in the lake.
Only one word will rhyme – yes! it's EGGS.

A thin hairy man of Belize
Got some strange-looking spots on his knees.
They spread to his thumb
Then all on his bum –
Look out – he's got a disease!

A Jew with muscles of steel
Let all of the girls have a feel.
But the night he was wed
His bride dropped down dead
'Cause none of his things turned out real.

A fat man from old Singapore
Said, 'My feet are terrible sore.'
The chiropodist said, 'Yes,
They're really quite red.
Try and keep the damned things off the floor.'

A highly trained old Russian spy
Was caught – so he started to cry.
They said, 'You've been a failure
From here to Australia.'
He said, 'Yes, but I try and I try.'

A man who fell down a mine
Said, 'Help! Someone drop me a line!'
Down came a letter
Saying *Hope you feel better,*
Dinner's at half-past nine.

A man from the Mull of Kintyre
Said, 'My bagpipes are always for hire.'
When he started to play
He was shot at, they say,
Which deflated them just like a tyre.

A cowboy out west in Montana
Had never seen a gymkhana.
He'd never seen fish
Or Lillian Gish,
An apple, a pan or banana.

The folks in Buckingham Palace
Bear nobody harm or malice.
Just like you and me,
They all watch TV.
All together now – DALLAS.

There was a young man from Berwick
Caught a 76 bus to Lewisham.
The conductor said, 'Get off.'
The man said, 'No.'
He will never get there this way.

A crow sitting up in a tree
Said, 'I'm black as a nigger, you see.
It wouldn't be right
If I were all white
Or even all Pak-i-stan-ee.'

A criminal in Rumania
To escape fled to distant Tasmania.
Police tried extradition
But friends signed a petition
Saying *No, he wants to remain here.*

A man who was asked out to dinner
Came back looking hungry and thinner.
He said, 'Don't look baffled,
The dinner was raffled
And somebody else was the winner.'

A chappie who came from New York
Tried to teach a parrot to talk.
But what a curse,
It worked in reverse,
Now *he* goes around going 'Squawk'.

The late Lord Louis Mountbatten
Spoke no languages, not even Latin.
Just a few words of French
At which people would blench
When they heard him say, 'Bring notre cat in.'

There was a young man of Penang
Who believed in letting things hang.
But one day when he sneezed
Something fell past his knees
And hit the floor with a clang.

A politico called Michael Foot
Said, 'This brush up the chimney I'll put.'
The tune he was humming
Was 'Christmas is Coming',
And so was a face full of soot.

There was an old man from Ghent
Who decided to live in a tent,
But when it started snowing
Said, 'I think I'll be going.'
He not only thought it – he went!

There was a young man called Mulgrew
Who contracted bronchitis and flu.
He got water on the brain
Again and again
So he died – so would I – wouldn't you?

A man called William J. Bind
Was stalking a stag and a hind
When a sound from his rear
Made him turn and, oh dear,
For there was a big bear behind.

A man who went out hunting bear
Said, 'Look, there's one over there!'
They chased it for weeks,
Over hills, lakes and creeks.
He was somewhere around, but where?

An old man from Hampstead Heath
Had a mouthful of terrible teeth.
Each tooth in his head
Was rotten or dead,
So the dentist just popped in a wreath.

A family man from Siberia
As a father was very inferior,
But one operation
Revised the situation
And now he's a Mother Superior.

An arsonist called Eric Ford
Wanted things he couldn't afford.
So later that night
Set his factory alight,
Then remembered . . . it wasn't insured!

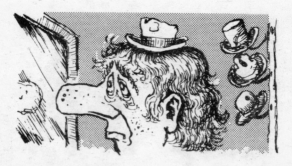

A man by the name of Fred
Had said, or is supposed to have said,
'I can't find a hat
To fit me and that
Is because of my ruddy great head.'

A scientist called Alger J. Hiss
To the Queen said, 'Ma'am, listen to this –
I've made three atom bombs
From old ladies' combs.
Come on now, Liz – give us a kiss.'

A Scotsman called Sandy McPhee
To the Queen said, 'Now listen to me.
I've just knitted a vest
From the hairs on my chest.
Ha' you got a kiss fer me?'

A man called Percival Lee
Got up one night for a wee.
When he got to the loo
It was twenty-to-two
But when he got back it was three.

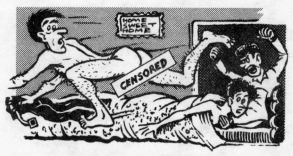

A locksmith from Barrow-on-Soar
Had affairs with women galore.
When caught *in flagrante*
In bed with his Auntie
He made a bolt for the door.

A fisherman from Cape Cod
Went around telling people, 'I'm God.'
His real name was Jim –
Alastair John McGinn –
But God he was certainly nod.

A man called Norvington Cole
Made a trip to Scott's hut at the Pole.
But when he got there
The cupboard was bare,
So he starved to death – poor soul.

For his daring aerial attacks
Von Richthofen won the Blue Max,
But! when Lieutenant Brown
Shot his plane down
He was the first to shout 'Pax!'

There was an illiterate Pole
Spoke one word of English, poor soul.
He spent every day
Watching football, they say –
For his one word of English was 'Goal!'

A man called Godfrey de Beers
Had a pair of enormous ears.
They stuck out from his head
Like the tomb of the dead
And they'd been like that for years.

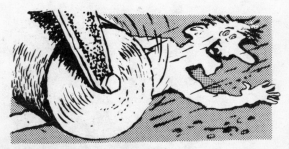

A man who was called Lucky Jim
Said, 'Away with all things that are grim.'
He stood in the street
Singing, 'Life can be sweet,'
And a steamroller ran over him.

A policeman on duty in Bow
Saw the traffic piled up in a row,
With the traffic lights dead
He just stood on his head
Shouting, 'On yer marks, ready, set, go!'

A knight called Sir Osbert de Nyde
Galloped into the town of Ryde.
But he just couldn't stop,
So – clippety clop –
He shot out the other side.

A house-auctioneer called Brown
Bought a semi-detached in the town
For his family of five,
Some dead, some alive,
At the last count three up and two down.

A doctor who made a prognosis
Said, 'Madam, 'tis my diagnosis
You have a touch
Of flu in the crutch.'
He was wrong – it was myxomatosis!

A lovely old lady from Skye
Couldn't sing but she said she would try,
Then she burst into song
But it didn't take long
Before somebody spat in her eye.

A lady called Shelagh Sinclair
Screamed as she leaped in the air,
She rushed from the loo
Shouting, 'Get away, shoo!
There's a bloody great spider in there!'

A young Jewish sailor called Nelson
('With a name like that you'll do well, son.')
He looked forward with glee
To a victory at sea –
So what was he doing in Belsen?

A convicted young thief called Milligan
Was paroled because he fell ill again,
So they let him away
But the very first day
He was caught with his hand in the till again.

A skarkling blin on the Glid
Went fracketing by in the nid,
But the wiggles took fright
Nor a brolikill bite
And the tater was grunney well rid.

A dirty old man at Pegu
To a girl said, 'I'm staring at you.'
'At me?' said she,
'Yes you,' said he,
'It's your knickers which I can see through!'

Said a man, 'Gad, I'm feeling terrific,
I've decided to swim the Pacific.'
But halfway on a reef
A cannibal chief
Ate him up – now I call that horrific.

When Gaugin went out to Tahiti
He shacked up with a twenty-stone sweetie.
When friends said to him,
'Can't you find someone thin?'
He said, 'Yes, but I like someone meatie.'

A tenor who liked Donizetti
Was told he was rotten and yet he
Yeti said, 'I'll now sing
The Wagnerian Ring,
But first – a plate of spaghetti.'

When washing the face of Big Ben
The hands hit a man cleaning X.
He complained to his boss,
He had to because
Twelve hours later it hit him again.

A man in the Bible once swore
A Martian had come to his door.
He went to the sink
Where he took a long drink,
Then widdled all over the floor.

A Scotsman who lived on the border
Wouldn't pay for the goods he would order.
When the bailiffs moved in
He just said with a grin,
'Aye! I'm meaner than Sir Harry Lauder.'

A ballerina from Riga
Said, 'I think I am losing my figa.'
She went on a diet
But to her disquiet
Got bigger and bigger and biga!

A man with a massive glass eye
Shot it out when he started to cry.
It fell in the dirt
Underneath a nun's skirt,
Looking straight up the poor woman's thigh.

A man who was driving a Jeep
Was trapped by a vast flock of sheep.
He beeped with his horn
Which they treated with scorn
Because sheep go 'Baa, Baa' not 'Beep, Beep'.

A coal-miner living in Wales
Bought his wife a fur coat in the sales.
It wasn't much fun
For the thing weighed a ton —
Very good in typhoons or in gales.

A man who went up to heaven
Arrived there at ten-past eleven.
When he knocked on the gate
Peter said, 'Sorry, mate,
We've closed till tomorrow at seven.'

A handyman from the Azores
Used to paint people's ceilings and floors.
He's done Auntie Kate's
And three of my mates',
He's done mine – now then, can he do yours?

In attempting to kill Rasputin
They tried poison, stabbing and shootin'.
When the man failed to die
They said, 'Just one more try,
Only this time try putting the boot in.'

FOR THE BEST IN PAPERBACKS, LOOK FOR THE

In every corner of the world, on every subject under the sun, Penguin represents quality and variety – the very best in publishing today.

For complete information about books available from Penguin – including Pelicans, Puffins, Peregrines and Penguin Classics – and how to order them, write to us at the appropriate address below. Please note that for copyright reasons the selection of books varies from country to country.

In the United Kingdom: For a complete list of books available from Penguin in the U.K., please write to *Dept E.P., Penguin Books Ltd, Harmondsworth, Middlesex, UB7 0DA*

In the United States: For a complete list of books available from Penguin in the U.S., please write to *Dept BA, Penguin, 299 Murray Hill Parkway, East Rutherford, New Jersey 07073*

In Canada: For a complete list of books available from Penguin in Canada, please write to *Penguin Books Canada Ltd, 2801 John Street, Markham, Ontario L3R 1B4*

In Australia: For a complete list of books available from Penguin in Australia, please write to the *Marketing Department, Penguin Books Australia Ltd, P.O. Box 257, Ringwood, Victoria 3134*

In New Zealand: For a complete list of books available from Penguin in New Zealand, please write to the *Marketing Department, Penguin Books (NZ) Ltd, Private Bag, Takapuna, Auckland 9*

In India: For a complete list of books available from Penguin, please write to *Penguin Overseas Ltd, 706 Eros Apartments, 56 Nehru Place, New Delhi, 110019*

In Holland: For a complete list of books available from Penguin in Holland, please write to *Penguin Books Nederland B.V., Postbus 195, NL–1380AD Weesp, Netherlands*

In Germany: For a complete list of books available from Penguin, please write to *Penguin Books Ltd, Friedrichstrasse 10 – 12, D–6000 Frankfurt Main 1, Federal Republic of Germany*

In Spain: For a complete list of books available from Penguin in Spain, please write to *Longman Penguin España, Calle San Nicolas 15, E–28013 Madrid, Spain*

FOR THE BEST IN PAPERBACKS, LOOK FOR THE

QUIZZES, GAMES AND PUZZLES

The Book Quiz Book   Joseph Connolly

Who was literature's performing flea . . .? Who wrote 'Live Now, Pay Later . . .'.? Keats and Cartland, Balzac and Braine, Coleridge conundrums, Eliot enigmas, Tolstoy teasers . . . all in this brilliant quiz book. You'll be on the shelf without it.

The Ultimate Trivia Game Book   Maureen and Alan Hiron

If you are immersed in trivia, addicted to quiz games, endlessly nosey, then this is the book for you: over 10,000 pieces of utterly dispensable information!

Unscrupulous?   Albie Fiore

Do you and your friends have principles? *Unscrupulous?* will help you to find out. A book of moral choices and decision-making that will turn friends into enemies, marriages into divorces and provide hours and hours of entertainment.

Plus four new trivia quiz books:
The Royalty Game
The TV Game
The Travel Game
The Pop Game

Crossword Books to baffle and bewilder

Eleven Penguin Books of The *Sun* Crossword
Eight Penguin Books of the *Sunday Times* Crossword
Seven Penguin Books of *The Times* Crossword
and
Four Jumbo Books of The *Sun* Crosswords

The First Penguin Book of *Daily Express* Crosswords
The Second Penguin Book of *Daily Express* Crosswords

Penguin Crossword Books – something for everyone, however much or little time you have on your hands.

BIOGRAPHY AND AUTOBIOGRAPHY IN PENGUIN

Jackdaw Cake   Norman Lewis

From Carmarthen to Cuba, from Enfield to Algeria, Norman Lewis brilliantly recounts his transformation from stammering schoolboy to the man Auberon Waugh called 'the greatest travel writer alive, if not the greatest since Marco Polo'.

Catherine   Maureen Dunbar

Catherine is the tragic story of a young woman who died of anorexia nervosa. Told by her mother, it includes extracts from Catherine's diary and conveys both the physical and psychological traumas suffered by anorexics.

Isak Dinesen, the Life of Karen Blixen   Judith Thurman

Myth-spinner and storyteller famous far beyond her native Denmark, Karen Blixen lived much of the Gothic strangeness of her tales. This remarkable biography paints Karen Blixen in all her sybiline beauty and magnetism, conveying the delight and terror she inspired, and the pain she suffered.

The Silent Twins   Marjorie Wallace

June and Jennifer Gibbons are twenty-three year old identical twins, who from childhood have been locked together in a strange secret bondage which made them reject the outside world. *The Silent Twins* is a real-life psychological thriller about the most fundamental question – what makes a separate, individual human being?

Backcloth   Dirk Bogarde

The final volume of Dirk Bogarde's autobiography is not about his acting years but about Dirk Bogarde the man and the people and events that have shaped his life and character. All are remembered with affection, nostalgia and characteristic perception and eloquence.

Penguins are proud to publish
the Greatest War Memoirs in the history of
the English-speaking people

Adolf Hitler: My Part in His Downfall
Bathos, pathos, gales of drunken laughter, and insane military
goonery explode in superlative Milliganese.

'Rommel?' 'Gunner Who?'
More Milligan military mania, but with a few Desert Rats thrown
in for good measure!

Monty: His Part in My Victory
The Nineteenth Battery forge into Tunis, cocksure and carefree
as the Milligan memoirs roll on . . .

Mussolini: His Part in My Downfall
Britannia rules the waves, but sometimes she waives the rules,
and Spike is set to liberate – *gasp* – Italy.

Where Have All the Bullets Gone?
In response to pressing – and final? – demand from the Inland
Revenue, the fifth – and final? – volume of Mr Milligan's inimicable
war memoirs.

Goodbye, Soldier
The absolutely, utterly and completely last volume of Spike's
autobiography – for the time being.

'There is no one living and, with the exception of Groucho Marx,
no one dead, to match him at his best' – *Observer*

Also by Spike Milligan in Penguins:

Silly Verse for Kids
Small Dreams of a Scorpion
Transports of Delight
Further Transports of Delight
*Unspun Socks from a Chicken's
   Laundry*
There's a Lot of It About
Puckoon